Emily Faithfull

Poems

An Offering to Lancashire

Emily Faithfull

Poems
An Offering to Lancashire

ISBN/EAN: 9783744771603

Printed in Europe, USA, Canada, Australia, Japan

Cover: Foto ©Thomas Meinert / pixelio.de

More available books at **www.hansebooks.com**

POEMS:

An Offering to Lancashire.

PRINTED AND PUBLISHED FOR THE ART EXHIBITION FOR THE
RELIEF OF DISTRESS IN THE COTTON DISTRICTS.

LONDON:

EMILY FAITHFULL,

Printer and Publisher in Ordinary to Her Majesty,

VICTORIA PRESS, 83A, FARRINGDON STREET, E.C.

1863.

PREFACE.

THE task of seeing this little volume through the press has been an easy and pleasant one. Most of the contributions have been written specially and many more might have been added but for the wish that the book should appear at Christmas, and the brief time consequently allowed for its preparation. Miss Faithfull undertook to print and publish a thousand copies free of expense, the compositors of the Victoria Press volunteering their services, and Messrs. Richard Herring & Co. furnishing the paper gratuitously, so that the proceeds of the sale will be devoted to the object to which the volume is dedicated.

ISA CRAIG.

CONTENTS.

POEMS:

An Offering to Lancashire.

SONNET.

WHAT is the work, the duty of the hour?
THIS, surely, chief:—to turn these ills to good:
Out of sour poison draw the wholesome food;
Chasing ill thoughts that sever rich and poor.
Oh! could we feel that every open'd door
Made way to HEARTS! drove out the spectral brood
Of dark distrustings—so that now we stood
At one in spirit—One for evermore!
Is this too much? yet register the vow,
Ye faithful Labourers! not to lose your hold;
The bars once broken, still to keep them so;
Then the fresh page in Life's great book unrolled,
With eyes made clear to read it, shall repay
With tenfold good the sorrow of to-day.

EMILY TAYLOR.

B

A ROYAL PRINCESS.

I, a princess, king-descended, stuck with jewels, gilded,
    dressed,
Would rather be a peasant with her baby at her breast,
For all I shine so like the sun, and am purple like the west.

Two and two my guards behind, two and two before,
Two and two on either hand, they guard me evermore;
Me, poor dove that must not coo—eagle that must not soar.

All my fountains cast up perfumes, all my gardens grow
Scented woods and foreign spices, with all flowers in blow
That are costly, out of season as the seasons go.

All my walls are lost in mirrors whereupon I trace
Self to right hand, self to left hand, self in every place,
Selfsame solitary figure, selfsame seeking face.

Then I have an ivory chair high to sit upon,
Almost like my Father's chair, which is an ivory throne:
There I sit uplift and upright, there I sit alone.

Alone by day, alone by night, alone days without end;
My Father and my Mother give me treasures, search and
spend :—
O my Father, O my Mother, have you ne'er a friend?

As I am a lofty princess, so my Father is
A lofty king, accomplished in all kingly subtilties,
Holding in his strong right hand world-kingdoms' balances.

He has quarrelled with his neighbours, he has scourged
his foes;
Vassal counts and princes follow where his pennon goes,
Long-descended valiant lords whom the vulture knows.

On whose track the vulture swoops, when they ride in state
To break the strength of armies and topple down the great :
Each of these my courteous servant, none of these my mate.

My Father counting up his strength sets down with equal pen
So many head of cattle, head of horses, head of men:
These for slaughter, these for breeding, with the how and
when

Some to work on roads, canals, some to man his ships;
Some to smart in mines beneath sharp overseers' whips;
Some to trap fur-beasts in lands where utmost winter nips.

Once it came into my heart and whelmed me like a flood,
That these too are men and women, human flesh and blood;
Men with hearts and men with souls tho' trodden down
    like mud.

All that day I sat alone, would not eat nor drink,
Sat humiliated down in dust to weep and think:
My heart grew like a stone; I felt it sink and sink and
    sink.

At night my Father held a banquet: I must needs be
    there,
Statue-cold, severe, and stately, if not statue-fair;
With hereditary jewels clustered in my hair,

With a fan of rainbow feathers and a golden chain,
Some bore gusty lights before me, some bore up my train:
"These are men, are men, are men," throbbed my heart
    and brain.

Our feasting was not glad that night, our music was
    not gay;
On my Mother's graceful head I marked a thread of grey,
My Father frowning at the fare seemed every dish to weigh.

I sat beside them sole princess in my exalted place,
My ladies and my gentlemen stood by me on the dais:
A mirror showed me I look old and haggard in the face;

It showed me that my ladies all are fair to gaze upon,
Plump, plenteous-haired, to every one love's secret lore
    is known,
They laugh by day, they sleep by night: ah me, what
    is a throne?

The singing men and women sang that night as usual,
The dancers danced in pairs and sets; but music had a fall,
A melancholy windy fall as at a funeral.

Amid the toss of torches to my chamber back we swept;
My ladies loosed my golden chain; meantime I could
    have wept
To think of one that was not loosed whether I waked
    or slept.

I took my bath of scented milk delicately waited on,
They burned sweet things for my delight, cedar and
    cinnamon,
They lit my shaded silver lamp and left me there alone.

A day went by, a week went by; and next I heard it said:
"Men are clamouring, women, children, clamouring to be fed;
"Men, like famished dogs, are howling in the streets for
    bread."

So two whispered by my door, not thinking I could hear,
Vulgar, naked truth, ungarnished for a royal ear;
Fit for hustling in the background, not to stalk so near.

But I strained my utmost sense to catch this truth and
    mark :—
"There are families out grazing like cattle in the park."—
"A pair of peasants must be saved, even if we build an ark."

A merry jest, a merry laugh; each strolled upon his way:
One was my page, a pretty lad, in dress perhaps too gay;
One was my youngest maid, as sweet and white as cream
    in May.

Other footsteps followed softly with a weightier tramp;
Voices said: "Picked soldiers have been summoned from
the camp,
"To quell these base-born ruffians who make free to howl
and stamp."

"Howl and stamp?" one answered: "They made free
to hurl a' stone
"At the minister's state coach, well aimed and stoutly
thrown."
"There's work then for the soldiers, for this rank crop
must be mown."

"One I saw, a poor old fool, with ashes on his head,
"Whimpering because a girl had snatched his crust of bread:
"Then he dropped; when some one raised him, it turned
out he was dead."

"After us the deluge," was retorted with a laugh:
"If bread's the staff of life they must walk without a
staff."—
"While I've a loaf they're welcome to my blessing and the
chaff."—

These passed.   The King : stand up.   Said my Father
    with a smile :
" Daughter mine, your Mother comes to sit with you awhile,
" She's sad to-day ; and who but you her sadness can
    beguile ? "

He too left me.   Shall I touch my harp now whilst I wait,—
I hear them doubling guard below before our palace gate—
Or shall I work the last gold stitch into my veil of state;

Or shall my woman stand and read some unimpassioned scene,
There's music of a lulling sort in words that pause
    between ;
Or shall she merely fan me while I wait here for the
    Queen ?

Again I caught my Father's voice in sharp word of
    command :
"Charge,"—a clash of steel :—" Charge again, the rebels
    stand :
" Smite and spare not, hand to hand ; smite and spare
    not, hand to hand."

There swelled a tumult at the gate, high voices waxing
    higher ;
A flash of red reflected light lit the Cathedral spire ;
I heard a cry for faggots, then I heard a yell for fire.

" Sit and roast there with your meat, sit and bake there
    with your bread,
"You who sat and saw us starve," one shrieking woman said:
" Sit on your throne and roast with your crown upon your
    head."

O Queen my Mother, come in haste; yet is your haste too slack;
I have set my face towards where there is no looking back,
I have set my foot upon the unreturning track.

This thing will I do whilst my Mother tarrieth :
I will take my fine spun gold, but not to sew therewith ;
I will take my gold and gems, and rainbow fan and
    wreath ;

With a ransom in my lap, a king's ransom in my hand,
I will go down to these people, will stand face to face ;
    will stand
Where they curse King, Queen and Princess of this
    cursed land.

They shall take all to buy them bread, take all I have
    to give ;
I, if I perish, perish ; they to-day shall eat and live ;
I, if I perish, perish ; that's the goal, I half conceive :

Once to stand up face to face with heart-pulse loud and
    hot—
It may be in this latter day I stand thus in my lot—
And cry : "I love you, love you," to those who know
    me not ;

Once to speak before the world, rend bare my heart
    and show
This lesson I have learned which is death, is life, to
    know.
I, if I perish, perish.   In the Name of God I go.

                      CHRISTINA G. ROSSETTI.

SACRIFICE.

2 Timothy i. xii.

ALL, all I've given, I've given my All to God;
Joy, Love, the bright career wherein I trod;
Bound them to regions more than Earth sublime,
Deferr'd them to an hour more fixed than Time.
"I am persuaded He can keep them All,"
And give me back each one from forth their Pall
Brighter than I resign them, mine at last,
When this sad Present shall be chang'd to Past.

I shall be happy then, with all the Power
Of all the Anguish of this bitter Hour;
I shall possess each Earth-abandoned Hope;
Grow free to roam wherever Will hath scope;
Ambition will content each high desire,
And Joy and Love burn with a Spirit's Fire.

V.

IN THE WINTER.

In the winter flowers are springing,
  In the winter woods are green,
Where our banished birds are singing,
  Where our summer sun is seen.
Our cold midnights are coeval
  With an evening and a morn
Where the forest gods hold revel
  And the spring is newly born.

While the earth is full of fighting,
  While men rise and curse their day,
While the foolish strong are smiting
  And the foolish weak betray,
The true hearts behind are growing,
  The brave spirits work alone,
Where love's summer wind is blowing
  In a truth-irradiate zone.

While we cannot shape our living
  To the beauty of our skies,
While man wants though earth is giving,
  Nature calls but man denies,
How the old worlds round Him gather
  Where their Maker is their Sun!
How the children know the Father
  Where the will of God is done!

Daily woven with our story,
  Sounding far above our strife,
Is a time-enclosing glory,
  Is a space-absorbing life.
We can dream no dream Elysian,
  There is no good thing might be,
But some angel has the vision,
  But some human soul shall see.

Is thy strait horizon dreary?
  Is thy foolish fancy chill?
Change the feet that have grown weary
  For the wings that never will.

IN THE WINTER.

There are kingdoms for the spirit
  Beyond worlds and ages far,
Thou hast all things to inherit
  And a joy in every star.

G. E. M.

THE THREE HORSES.

WHAT shall I be? I will be a knight,
   Walled up in armour black;
With a sword of sharpness, a hammer of might,
   And a spear that will not crack;
So black, so blank, in the wood no light
   Shall glimmer from my track.

So saddle my coal-black steed, my men,
   Which Ravenwing I call;
For the night is rising from the fen,
   And the sky is like a pall;
And out of the dark, and out of the den,
   The bad things gather all.

Let him go!—let him go! Let him plunge!—Keep away!
   He's a foal of Night's own brood.
Like a skeleton-horse, in his gaunt array,
   With poitrel and frontlet good,
Spectre-ridden, he bounds away
   To the heart of the midnight wood.

Woe to the thing that checks our force,
    That meets us in our gear!
Giant, enchanter, devil, or worse,
    He goes down before my spear.
I and Ravenwing on the course—
    Let all the wicked fear!

Between the trees with a clank I ride—
    But the goblins flit to and fro.
From the skull of darkness, deep and wide,
    The eyes of the dragons glow;
From the thickets the silent serpents glide;
    But I pass them—I let them go.

For I shall come, ere the morning light,
    On some child that cries alone;
On some noble knight o'ermatched in fight,
    Outbreathed, and all but gone;
Or I spur to a half-seen glimmer white,
    And a half-heard lady's moan.

I bear the child, as in a nest,
    'Twixt sheltering wings of steel;
I bear him home to his mother's breast,

And her tears my triumph seal;
And his tiny hand, in my gauntlet pressed,
   Like a lingering thanks I feel.

And spur in flank, and lance in rest,
   On the old knight's foes I flash;
And scatter the knaves to east and west,
   With clang and tumult and crash;
I leave them the law, as they learn it best,
   In bruise, and breach, and gash.

And the lady I lift to my saddle-bow,
   And I never ask the tale;
Her trembling heart grows quiet and slow;
   She slumbers against my mail;
Home to my mother's bower we go,
   Where a welcome will not fail.

Home through the wood and the evil night,
   Where glow the dragons' eyes,
Where wander the lawless men of might,
   And the goblin-things arise;
Home like a knight that loves the right,
   And will strike for it till he dies.

c

Alas! 'tis a boy's wild dream—that is all :
  In the fens no dragons blow ;
Into giants' hands no ladies fall ;
  Through the forest wide roadways go.
If I love a maiden, and ever shall,
  My love I cannot show.

I will not saddle old Ravenwing ;
  I will not ride by night ;
No spectre would cross my galloping,
  But the moonbeams long and white ;
And the birds from their quiet slumbering,
  Would flit off an arrow's flight.

But bridle me Twilight, my dapple-gray,
  With a snaffle rein and bit ;
Let a youth bring him round to the door, I say,
  As the shadows begin to flit ;
Just as the darkness dreams into day,
  And the owls begin to sit.

And all the armour I will wear
  Is a sword, like the first blue gray,
That to right and left doth mow and share

The grisly darkness away
From the gates of the morning, still and fair,
  By which walks out the day.

I leave the arched forest grim,
  And into the broad land ride.
The torrent is deep—we plunge and swim.
  The cold light wets the tide,
From the opening east, like the plashes dim
  On my Twilight's dappled side.

We pass like morn o'er dale and hill,
  O'er desert, moor, and beach;
In the market-places he stands still,
  And I lift my voice and preach;
Like waters men flow and gather, until
  Ten thousand men I teach.

For I speak of justice, I speak of truth,
  Of law and of social wrong;
And my words are moulded by right and ruth,
  Into a solemn song;
And the upturned faces of age and youth
  Gather the cadence long.

They bring me causes from all the land,
  That strife may be forgot;
The balance will swerve to neither hand;
  The poor I favour not.
If a man withstand, out sweeps my brand—
  I slay him upon the spot.

Alas, my sword! What! I to slay
  Perchance a better than I!
My hands have not been clean alway
  And my sin it is too nigh.
I will not ride the dapple-gray;
  In the stable let him lie.

I dare not judge, I dare not kill;
  The sword I will not wear.
A better service remaineth still—
  Good tidings I will bear.
As the light climbs up the noontide hill,
  Bring round my snow-white mare.

Take heed, my men, that from crest to heel
  She has neither spot nor speck.
No shining bit her mouth shall feel,

No tightening rein her neck;
No saddle-girth, with buckles of steel,
　Her mighty breathing check.

Lay on her a cloth of silver sheen;
　Bring me a robe of white;
For all the way we shall be seen
　By the shining of the light—
A glimmering glory in forests green,
　A star on the mountain-height.

Like a horse of heaven, with a joyous bound,
　Forth to the wind she leaps;
Full-filled of light, she skims the ground;
　Then, lapt in the forest-deeps,
A torrent of shadows, without a sound,
　Over her ripples and sweeps.

And the sun and the wind are life and love.
　Where the serpent slimed the bark,
Broods the silent, the shining dove.
　Where dragons breathed the dark,
Glad troops of children, below, above,
　Gather with hollo and hark.

It is joy, it is joy, to ride the world
  With a message of love and bliss!
Many a white flag has been unfurled,
  But never a flag like this—
The mane of my mare by the glad winds curled,
  In joy's own wantonness.

And maidens look up, with eyes of light,
  From the nooks where wild flowers meet;
And the ripened fruit falls ruddy and bright,
  Like jewels, at their feet,
As I gallop by on my mare so white,
  Through the dappling shadows fleet.

For I have a message of might and mirth—
  The dawn of another morn.
I go to bear the news of birth
  Through city and land of corn.
Gracious gladness shall clothe the earth,
  For a child, a child is born.

But what means the message—*A child is born?*
  It means that the earth grows young;
That the heart, with sin and sorrow torn,

Shall be whole and happy and strong;
That the fountain of sighing, and fear, and scorn,
Shall break into bubbling song.

Is this all? Ah! no. The message saith,
That the spirit no more shall pine;
That Self shall die an ecstatic death,
And be born a thing divine;
That God's own joy and God's own breath
Shall fill man like living wine.

That ambition shall vanish, and love be king;
And pride lower and lower lie;
Till, for very love of a living thing,
A man would forget—and die;
Were it not that love is the very spring
That all life is living by.

Alas! is it this? What a fool am I—
In the kingdom of heaven the least—
To choose a labour so lowly-high,
To anoint myself a priest!
In the worst of prides—that I might sit by
The Master of the feast.

Alas! alas!　Lead her back again.
　Some healthful sorrow I need.
I am overweening, ignorant, vain.
　Yet, Lord, if I take good heed,
May I wash the hoofs and comb the mane
　Of the shining gospel-steed?

GEORGE MACDONALD.

SUDDEN LIGHT.

I HAVE been here before,
  Though when or how I cannot tell;
I know the path beyond the door,
  The sweet fresh smell,
The sighing sound, the lights around the shore.

You have been mine before,
  How long ago I do not know:
But just when, at that swallow's soar,
  Your neck turned so,
Some veil did fall, I knew it all of yore.

Before may be again:
  Oh! press my eyes into your neck.
Shall we not be for ever lain
  Thus for Love's sake,
And sleep, and wake, yet never break the chain.

D. G. ROSSETTI.

D

FOUR SONNETS FROM EARLY ITALIAN PICTURES.

VERSIFIED IN ENGLISH BY WILLIAM BELL SCOTT.

I.

INSCRIBED ON THE PICTURE OF "DIO PADRE" IN THE CAMPO SANTO, PISA, BY MASTER PIETRO DI BARTOLO, 1390.

ALL ye who look upon this picture, see
   Our high God, our most pitiful Creator,
Who numbered, measured, weighed, all things that be,
   Working with love; who also made the store
Of ninefold splendours, in whose harmony
   The angel natures agitate; by whom,
Himself immovable, all things are moved—
   Shaped fair at first, whate'er they have become.
Open your spiritual eyes and be reproved,
   Considering well the ordinance of all,
Praising the hand which framed so wonderful
   This world, and that to which we hope the call
Of time will bring us when our years are full,
   To walk in Paradise with angels tall.
Even to this aspires my pictured story,
To show the depth beneath, the middle way, the Glory.

II.

Verses beneath the Picture Emblematical of the City of Siena, in the Palazzo Pubblico there, by Ambrogio di Lorenzo, 1339.

When laurelled Honour in the hall holds sway,
    Making as one the many minds of men,
Subduing each and strengthening all, till they
    The commonweal as their just Lord maintain,
The State is strong, and peaceful outwardly
    Lives in her children's good; her great eyes bent
Upon the starry splendours constantly
    Revolving round her in a firmament
Where Virtues are the planets. At her feet
    The Signorie with tribute, tax, and due,
All willing offerings, from the four ways meet;
    And Justice is all-seeing, winged, and true;
And Dame Civility, by days and nights
Adds to the common stores of uses, wants, delights.

III.

ON THE PICTURE 'OF GOOD GOVERNMENT, A PORTION OF THE SAME
WALL PAINTING AS THE LAST.

TURN your considerate eyes here, ye who reign,
And note what hath been figured on this wall.
A goddess crownèd with great excellence
Renders to every one his amplest gain:
Behold from her how many good things fall;
Behold sweet Peace the flowers of life dispense
Over the city which this goddess serves;
Behold she guards and watches, yea she feeds
And cherishes all those whom honour leads
Within her gates: for her eye never swerves,
But like the sun that everywhere surveys,
Illumines him who justly merits praise,
Sustains the weak, and sends on the evil, rain
Of cleansing fire and retributive pain.

IV.

VERSES UNDER THE CORONATION OF THE VIRGIN, BY SANO DI PIETRO, IN THE PALAZZO PUBBLICO, AT SIENA, PAINTED 1445.

VERY glorious throughout heaven! in one,
Mother, maid, spouse: (by greatest mystery she
Who was the daughter of her unborn Son:
She whom the Father from eternity
Found humble more than any other maid,
And gave her of this universe the crown:)
Here have I, Sano Pietro, essayed
To paint, unworthy of such high renown.
Thou, Virgin-mother of immaculate God,
Crowned by His terrible holy hand, look down
Upon the field, the vineyard, and the town,
Guard them from fire and sword, and from the rod
Of pestilence and other ills; for we,
Crying, Ave! gratia plena! trust in thee.

AFTER SUNSET.

The vast and solemn company of clouds
Around the Sun's death, lit, incarnadined,
Cool into ashy wan; as Night enshrouds
The level pasture, creeping up behind
Through voiceless vales, o'er lawn and purpled hill
And hazèd mead, her mystery to fulfil.
Cows low from far-off farms; the loitering wind
Sighs in the hedge, you hear it if you will;
Though all the wood, alive atop with wings
Lifting and sinking through the leafy nooks,
Seethes with the clamour of ten thousand rooks.
Now every sound at length has dropt away.
These few are sacred moments. One more Day
Drowned in the shadowy gulf of bygone things.

W. Allingham.

THE MERSEY AND THE IRWELL.

SUGGESTED BY A VERY CURIOUS AND INTERESTING MODEL OF THE
LITTLE TOWN OF LIVERPOOL, AS IT EXISTED IN THE EARLIER
PART OF THE LAST CENTURY.

A CENTURY since the Mersey flowed
  Unburdened to the sea;
In the blue air no smoky cloud
  Hung over wood and lea,
Where the old church with the fretted tower
  Had a hamlet round its knee.

And all along the Eastern way
  The sheep fed on the track;
The grass grew quietly all the day,
  Only the rooks were black;
And the pedlar frightened the lambs at play
  With his knapsack on his back.

Where blended Irk and Irwell streamed
  While Britons pitched the tent,
Where legionary helmets gleamed,
  And Norman bows were bent,

An ancient shrine was once esteemed
  Where pilgrims daily went.

A century since the pedlar still
  Somewhat of this might know,
Might see the weekly markets fill
  And the people ebb and flow
Beneath St. Mary's on the hill
  A hundred years ago.

Since then a vast and filmy veil
  Is o'er the landscape drawn,
Through which the sunset hues look pale,
  And grey the roseate dawn,
And the fair face of hill and dale
  Is apt to seem forlorn.

Smoke rising from a thousand fires
  Hides all that past from view;
Vainly the prophet's heart aspires,
  It hides the future too;
And the England of our slow-paced sires
  Is thought upon by few.

Yet man lives not by bread alone,—
  How shall he live by gold?
The answer comes in a sudden moan
  Of sickness, hunger, and cold;
And lo! the seed of a new life sown
  In the ruins of the old!

The human heart, which seemed so dead,
  Wakes with a sudden start;
To right and left we hear it said
  "Nay; 'tis a noble heart,"
And the angels whisper overhead
  "There's a new shrine built in the mart!"

And though it be long since daisies grew
  Where Irk and Irwell flow,
If human love springs up anew,
  And angels come and go,
What matters it that the skies were blue
  A hundred years ago!

BESSIE R. PARKES.

E

THE EYE OF GOD.

ALL creation liveth
  In the eye of God ;
Kings that rule the nations,
  Flowers that deck the sod.

All creation liveth
  In that Eye, whose lid
Never droops in slumber ;
  From which nought is hid.

Nought that eye o'erlooketh,
  Motes of life too small
For man's aided vision—
  God's eye sees them all !

Everywhere, and always,
  Now and heretofore,
Where no line hath sounded,
  Where no thought can soar ;

God's great eye is open;
  God's eye looketh through,
Seeing, comprehending
  What all tendeth to.

Nought that Eye withstandeth;
  Its keen shafts of sight,
Like electric arrows
  Cleave the depths of night.

Thou canst not enshroud thee
  In a pall so dense,
But God's eye hath tracked thee,
  And will draw thee thence.

God is with thee, round thee,
  God's great eye is set,
On thee like the meshes
  Of a wondrous net.

There is no escaping!—
  Death but brings thee nigher;
Lays thee still more open
  To His glance of fire!

Yet fear not—but rather
   Let thy soul rejoice
That God's Omnipresence,
   Is beyond thy choice.

That from the All-Seeing
   Nought can thee remove ;
For that ceaseless vision,
   That great Eye, is LOVE !

MARY HOWITT.

AD SEPULCRUM.

A FRAGMENT.

His plumy helm he laid aside,
  Agnes! Agnes!
Here he doff'd his knightly pride,
  Sister! Agnes!

His knees on the sod he leant,
  Where thou art sleeping:
His brows to the cross he bent,
  Bitterly weeping.

The gusts, that made the branches moan—
  Betroth'd Agnes!
Pierc'd his bosom always lone—
  Betray'd Agnes!

Billow-like swell'd the grief
  Over his heart anew:
Prone to the ground he fell,
  Like a cold corse in hue.

Word of grief none he spoke :
Deep was his groaning.
There should his heart have broke
Tow'rd an atoning.

Up ! he'll fight in Palestina,
Bare of his dishonour'd helm,
He that left thine head uncover'd
Unto scorns that overwhelm.

There on grappled flag the dying
Templars set
Strained eyeballs,—and their flying
Souls forget.

There the horsehoofs, rearing wildly,
Burst the pikemen's kneeling line
Ere the scimitar-waving rider
Sinks by cross-bow shaft supine.

Under the fallen steed,
Cloven in twain his arm,
Over the slain his head,
Feet on the groaning warm.

Pass'd by the flying rout,
  In the still night alone,
By the chill dews awak'd,
  Stiff as the quarry-stone.

In the solitude of the many dead,
  From the bonds of numbness and of pain,
From oblivion craved and coveted,
  Let to conscience wake his heart again.

Saying, How shall he enter where
  Christ in all time is view'd?
Faith is unbroken there,
  Love is not lewd.

Ah, Christ! that I could breathe her tale
  Yet once more in his ears!
To the proud man's eyes before he dies
  Should come again thick tears.

She twin'd herself a chaplet
  Of the white may and the red;
She twin'd herself her chaplet,
  Then tore it from her head.

She gather'd her five branches
  Of the red may and the white ;
They grac'd her hands of rose and milk—
  Full goodly was the sight.

She came across that little bridge
  Above the brawling rill ;
She wrapt her kerchief round her breast,
  For the wind was loud and chill.

Then bruisèd she the blossoms
  Of white and crimson may ;
Some she gave to the whistling wind,
  To carry them where he may.

Some she let from her soft hands fall,
  And flutter down into the brook :
As the waters carried them under the bridge
  She follow'd with vacant look.

That swelling stream discoloured
  Their white and crimson glow :
As the water sank in the delicate leaves,
  They seem'd to melt like snow.

Then took she those may-branches
  That had been so pure and sweet:
And shook off the thin and pining flowers,
  And trampled them under her feet.

"And oh, like those boughs of may," she cried,
  "Was the morning of life to me:
Hopes and schemes as thick and as bright
  As the blossoms hang on the tree.

"Some have I given to the whistling wind,
  To carry them where he may,
And some into the brook let fall—
  And the waters have borne them away.

"Some have I trampled under my feet,
  With bitter thoughts and ill ;
And the flower of flowers a deceiver I gave:
  One trust is left me still."

She look'd adown into the brook,
  Her tears in the dark stream fell:
Her bosom was cold, heart heavy as lead,
  And the wind was chill and snell.

She let her arms beside her fall,
  Laid her brow to the cold grey stone:
She bow'd in her sobs to the low bridge wall,
  And her gaze on the ground was thrown.

When she lifted her brow from the cold grey stone
  She gather'd those boughs of may:
One branch gather'd she out of the five
  And went on her lonesome way.

When she came to the green fair bank,
  The sun gleam'd over the hill:
The round rain-drop on her cheek had fall'n
  When she looked in the brawling rill.

There she planted the branch of may
  Whose blossoms were scatter'd and strown,
All in the grass and the green soft moss—
  And her gaze on the ground was thrown.

All in the grass and the green soft moss
  She planted it, right as is meet—
"God prosper thee with sunshine and rain,
  And guard thee from wayfaring feet.

"For now to the nunnery yonder
  My steps by his grave I have bent.
There must I rue my sinful life
  And love too lightly lent.

"All my days of fair fame are over;
  All my wealth I carry with me;
I thought to have shared it with my false lover—
  Now I give to this nunnerie.

"Even as thou, poor bruisèd branch,
  God thee giving sunshine and rain,
Mayst yet rise to a noble thorn
  Though I see thee never again.

"I go seeking sweet hope and peace,
  To win for a fairer morrow,
And the love, which a sinful heart despised,
  To regain with prayer and sorrow."

                              C. B. CAYLEY.

BROTHERS.

I.

HARD is the lot of the worker :
His heart had need be brave,
With death in life to wrestle
From the cradle to the grave.
Sternly the sorrows meet·him
In the thick of the mortal fray—
But the night must serve for weeping—
Work must be done by day.

High rose the houses, a great human hive,
Crowded from roof to base with busy life.
While in the stifling courts the children swarmed.
A chill, grey day died blank and colourless
Within the narrow walls that hedged a home,
Amid those close-pent dwellings, as out-worn
A twice-made mother, on the bed of birth,
Trembled her life away.

The light was gone;
And the poor chamber held the pomp of death—
More awful than the majesty of Kings—
Before set free from labour, to his home

The father came   And first there greeted him
Faint cries of new-found life, and then he passed
Into that silent presence.

                              From his sight
The nurse, a simple neighbour, bore the babe
And left him with his sorrow and the night.
Low in a corner lay his little lad,
Whose seven blythe years had brought no bitterness
Like this bad day's: for never in his pain
Had she been pitiless; nor, until now,
Unanswering to his cries.   For he had cried
"I'm hungry," and she had not stretched her hands;
"I'm weary," and she drew him not to rest,
With touch of tender kisses on his hair.
Now, wearied out with weeping wilderment,
He slept.

                Between the sleeping and the dead
The strong man bowed himself and took his place
To watch the night out.

                       Covered, still, and white,
It lay—that awful burden—on the bed
He should have shared.   He did not lift the shroud

To look upon the lifeless face, or press
Its lips with unfelt kisses ; did not stain
Its whiteness with a tear. Beside him lay
Her one ring—worn throughout those wedded years,
From fingers stiffening in the clasp of death
Withdrawn ; and as he gently lifted it,
A sudden strangeness fell on all his life,
And made it blank through all its soulless days,
But left, like hill-tops lifted thro' a flood,
The living hours of love.

                              The boy awoke
And saw him sit there ; slept, and woke again ;
And there he sat and loomed out of the dark
Until he seemed a giant to the child.
The chequered moonlight fell across the floor
Leaving the death-bed curtained by the dark
And awful mysteries of life and death,
Confused, impenetrable, undefined,
Hovered about the boy, and he would fain
Have called upon his father in the night,
But that he seemed a portion of the dread,
The unappeasable, appealless fate

That held him, and should hold him ever more.
Then he bethought him of his prayer, and said
"Our Father," and so slept until the dawn.
And in the faint dawn he was sitting there,
Who never once had drowsed nor drooped his head
Nor groaned for any anguish of his soul—
But when the morning sun looked in, he rose
With sweat drops on his forehead.

II.

He must serve needs of the body,
Let the soul's be served or not ;
And work must be remembered
Though God should be forgot.
Yet if God were forgotten
By weary women and men,
To the earth, however guilty,
He would come a child again.

The boy was nursed and named—a northern name—
Ronald—the rush of battle on the hills
It seemed to echo by the hearth of peace.
The father gave the elder brother charge

To shut out strangers, keep the child from harm,
And feed the fire upon the winter's hearth,
Himself performed the menial offices
Which humble women for their households do.
While in his bosom slept the little one,
And woke the woman's nature in the man
To do the woman's part, that if he stirred
Or moaned but in a dream of restlessness,
It roused him from the deepest sleep of toil,
New nerving every sense.
When summer came, Allen, the elder boy,
In a round bundle clasping Ronald fast,
Sat in a doorway in the steep old street
That thrid the thickest quarter of the town,
Yet went out freely to the breezy fields
That lay within the shadow of the hills.
Then, as his baby learnt to walk and run,
Farther and farther he would lead him forth
Beyond the streets; in the thick meadow grass
To find bright golden buttercups and nests
Of daisies silver-fringed.
Then, having learnt to read on winter nights,

He took the Pilgrim's Progress to the hills,
And read while little Ronald ran about,
Till hunger drove them home. And as the days
Lengthened and brightened, he, with pockets filled
With bread with which to feed the ravenous babe—
Who cried because he might not eat the book—
Stayed all day long abroad among the hills :
The hills to him were meanings of the book :
He saw the sunset redden on the rocks,
And climbing to a point where he could watch
The sun sink on the plain, before him lay
The deep dark river in a belt of cloud,
While the great glory of the golden towers
Of the celestial city rose beyond.
And in the night, when drunken revel roused
The echoing street, the boy would lie awake,
And firm resolve to go on pilgrimage :
His father should go with him, Ronald too :
Did they not dwell within that fearful place,
The City of Destruction ? And at length
One stifling night, when the court gasped for breath,
Wide-windowed, with a sudden thrilling cry,

F

There rose a rush of flame into the dark ;
There fell a sparkling shower of crimson fire ;
And all the gathering crowd amid the glare
Had demon faces. In his wild affright,
With passionate tears he seized his father's hand,
Beseeching him to flee. Then for a fool
His father chid him, while with wild delight
Ronald had clambered to his arms and clapped
His tiny hands and shouted when the crowd
Scattered before the fall of burning brands.
On Sabbath, to their haunts among the hills,
Allen and Ronald lured their father forth.
There, lying in the grass, he watched their play,
And learned at length to share it. Ronald loved
To play at burial: o'er his prostrate form
To heap up blade and blossom ruthless plucked,
And then to have his victim start to life,
Scattering the light load of the fragrant tomb.
Then o'er his heart a grateful sense of rest
And pleasant things provided all for play
Stole ; and on intervals of rest there rose
Strange questionings from childish lips, that reached

Unto the height of heaven, and went out
To the unmeasured bounds of Universe,
Till the man marvelled, feeling in his breast
The child-heart half renewed.

When suddenly——
His little Ronald, fever-smitten lay:
Moaning in suffering, or in passionate strength
Rising with crimson cheek and sparkling eyes
And hot clenched hands that battled as for life,
To sink back spent and helpless. How he watched
He worked not, slept not. He was almost fierce,
When, with unknowing eyes, the little one
Put him aside, and with a vehement clasp
Clung to his brother's neck. At length the fire
Burned itself out, and in its ashes left
The feeblest spark of life. The emaciate limbs
Lay quiet, and the thin blue veins spread cool
Over the wasted temples. As he watched
That healing night pass over him, he cried,
" God give him back, and lead me thus to Thee."
So learned he what was in the Father's heart,
And having learned, changed places with the child—

The fever smote him, and he bowed his head
With a strange meekness. A few days and nights
Confused and hurrying like his pulses faint,
Then a clear conscious passing of the soul
Through which the pang of parting keenly smote,
And the last hour was come. The children slept:
He gave no blessing, breathed no sad farewell—
He too would sleep and leave the world to God.

III.

Deep in the heart of the worker—
Too little understood—
Deep in the heart of the worker
Lies the sense of brotherhood.
Alone may sit the thinker,
And build his tower of thought ;
The earth's hard stone and iron
By many hands are wrought.

And from the hour when they woke fatherless,
There grew into the elder brother's life,
A deep and conscious sense of brotherhood—
That henceforth he must think, and toil, and bear,

For one who could not. So he took his place
Among the workers where the hundred wheels
That seem to weave the web of fate—go round.
And Ronald's nursing mother took the twain
To enrich herself, because she was so poor.
Thus patient years went on, and Ronald grew
Above his young companions, tall and strong.
And when at length it was his time to toil,
Went daily forth. His singing, as he went,
Even when the streets were grey and desolate
On rainy mornings woke the echoes up.
He was not selfish, yet was of the stuff
Through which that rust eats readiest; careless, gay,
With strong exuberant life; and most unlike
That pale and feeble brother, whose slight frame
Was swift to suffer, and whose keen strung nerves
Would find a very torture of the wheel
At times amid the noises of the mill.
He lived on books, and on the dew of dreams,
Cooled his hot thirst throughout the labouring day;
While every night he drank a living draught
From some full fount of thought to feed his dreams,

Night after night he sat down to the feast
Of knowledge with the poet and the sage:
The old magician science led him on
Beneath the strong foundations of the earth,
Through palaces enchanted; builded up
Invisibly, through ages; heaped with stores
Of treasures; floored with strange mosaic work
Of living forms extinguished: opened up
World upon world of wonder, order fair
Reigning through all; no loose disjointed dream,
But one vast, endless sequence and design,
Worthy the thought of God.

                 And wisdom came
And showed her glorious beauty to the youth,
Who thenceforth vowed to serve her evermore,
His rightful queen, whose subjects all are free.
Who freely must be chosen, crowned, obeyed,
Administ'ring the righteous laws of life,
All whose transgressors perish: are enslaved
By sin's strong fetters and the pangs of pain.
               Then he saw
His fellows working blindly in the yoke,

Becoming bond-slaves.   Where man serves the work
And not the work the man; if he escapes,
The hounds of famine hunt him back again ;
He lives but half his days, gives life itself
For th' lowest needs of life.
                            And sadder still
And sadder grew the spirit of the man
Within him.   Barren, if unshared
By these his fellows, seemed the richest fruit
Of wisdom.   Bitter even the bread of life.
And even Ronald shared not, but roamed forth
In search of action for each sense fresh roused
After the long day's dull monotony.
Till, on one night, flushed face and wandering eye
Met the pale student at the midnight hour,
Telling of fierce temptation.   Then a voice
Within him cried, commanding him to save.
And there arose a conflict in his soul
As from its depths an evil whisper rose—
"Am I my brother's keeper evermore ?"
And then he knew his lonely dreams were vain,
And all his life seemed walled up by despair.

Therefore his books were closed for many days ;
And Ronald, restless, and half conscience-struck,
Watched him and wondered that he did not speak ;
Till, sitting with his face hid in his hands,
One night he muttered almost with a groan,
"If I had only strength to work it out!"
And Ronald, turning on the threshold, cried,
"See, I have strength; it is strength this I feel!—
That drives me out each night to meet with men
Yet where's the use of it? I wish I were
The great blind wheel that sets the mill to work.
I know not what to do."

                       "Do this and live"
Rose like a prophet's speech to Allan's lips—
And they, though drifting more and more apart
Drew near and were at one as head and hand
As he unfolded what had been his thought
These many days. That fellow-workers might
So work together for their common weal;
So pour together in a common store
Those sacred gains of labour, which are life,
As to become the masters of themselves,

Masters and lords of their own heritage
Of labour.   And the work inspired the youth,
And going forth he gathered soon a band
Of eager fellow-labourers.   And the plan
Prospered, until the people owned the mill,
And not the mill the people.

                  Then new life
Came back to his old dreams and Allan dreamed
That from this newer, higher, freer life,
Men might rise up full furnished and complete
In all that makes the man, in strength and love ;
In knowledge and in wisdom and in worth.

                                 ISA CRAIG.

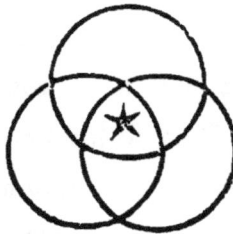

ENGLAND AND AMERICA.

1863.

We only know that in the sultry weather
  Men toiled for us as in the steaming room,
And in our minds we hardly set together
  The bondsman's penance and the freeman's loom.

We never thought the jealous Gods would store
  For us ill deeds of time-forgotten graves,
Nor heeded that the Mayflower one day bore
  A freight of Pilgrims, and another Slaves.

First on the bold upholders of the wrong,
  And last on us, the heavy laden years
Avenged the cruel triumphs of the strong—
  Trampled affections, and derided tears.

Labour degraded from her high behest
  Cries, "Ye shall know I am the living breath,

And not the curse of Man.   Ye shall have Rest—
The rest of famine and the rest of Death."

Oh, happy distant hours ! that shall restore
Honour to work, and pleasure to repose,
Hasten your steps, just heard above the roar
Of wildering passions and the crash of foes.

R. MONCKTON MILNES.

THE JESTER'S PLEA.

THE WORLD! Was jester ever in
  A viler than the present?
Yet if it ugly is . . . as sin,
  It almost is . . . as pleasant!
It is a merry world (*pro tem.*)
  And some are gay, and therefore
It pleases them—but some condemn
  The fun they do not care for.

It is an ugly world. Offend
  Good people—how they wrangle!
The manners that they never mend!
  The characters they mangle!
They eat, and drink, and scheme, and plod,
  And go to church on Sunday—
And many are afraid of God—
  And more of *Mrs. Grundy*.

The time for Pen and Sword was when
  " My ladye fayre," for pity
Could tend her wounded knight, and then
  Be tender for his ditty !
Some ladies now make pretty songs,—
  And some make pretty nurses :—
Some men are good for righting wrongs,—
  And some for writing verses.

One tax our patience long has stood—
  The tax that poets levy !—
I know the Muse is very good—
  I think she's rather heavy.
She now compounds for winning ways
  By morals of the sternest—
I think the bards of now-a-days
  Are painfully in earnest.

When Wisdom halts, I humbly try
  And put a point on Folly :
If Pallas won't be civil, I
  Away,—and flirt with Polly,—

Who quit the goddess for the maid
　　Must certainly be losers—
But Pallas is a lofty jade—
　　And beggars can't be choosers.

I do not wish to see the slaves
　　Of party, stirring passion,
Or psalms quite superseding staves,
　　Or piety "the fashion."
I bless the Hearts where pity glows,
　　Who here together banded
Are holding out a hand to those
　　That wait so empty-handed.

A righteous Work !—My masters, may
　　A jester by confession,
Scarce noticed join, half sad, half gay,
　　The close of your procession ;
The motley here seems out of place
　　With graver robes to mingle,
But if one tear bedews his face,
　　Forgive the bells their jingle.

FREDERICK LOCKER.

PRINTED BY EMILY FAITHFULL, VICTORIA PRESS, 83A, FARRINGDON STREET, E.C.

www.ingramcontent.com/pod-product-compliance
Lightning Source LLC
Chambersburg PA
CBHW021535270326
41930CB00008B/1267